MY LIFE AS A
BUDDHIST

FLEUR BRADLEY

45th Parallel Press

Published in the United States of America by Cherry Lake Publishing Group
Ann Arbor, Michigan
www.cherrylakepublishing.com

Editorial Consultant: Dr. Virginia Loh-Hagan, EdD, Literacy, San Diego State University
Content Adviser: Molly H. Bassett, Associate Professor and Chair in the Department of Religious Studies
   at Georgia State University
Reading Adviser: Beth Walker Gambro, MS, Ed., Reading Consultant, Yorkville, IL
Book Designer: Jen Wahi

Photo Credits: © coward_lion/istock, cover, 1; © Attasit saentep/Shutterstock, 4; © Kichigin/Shutterstock, 7;
   © Anthony Ricci/Shutterstock, 9; © ViDI Studio/Shutterstock, 10; © NDStock/Shutterstock, 13; © buraktumler/
   Shutterstock, 14; © Khanthachai C/Shutterstock, 17; © anek.soowannaphoom/Shutterstock, 18; ©Zakki
   Ahmada/Shutterstock, 22; ©Fakhri Anindita/Shutterstock, 24; © Ekapong/Shutterstock, 26; ©nuttavut
   sammongkol/Shutterstock, 28; © Roman Samborskyi/Shutterstock, 30

45th Parallel Press is an imprint of Cherry Lake Publishing Group.

Library of Congress Cataloging-in-Publication Data

Names: Bradley, Fleur, author.
Title: My life as a Buddhist / by Fleur Bradley.
Description: Ann Arbor : Cherry Lake Publishing, 2022. | Series: How the world worships
Identifiers: LCCN 2021039873 | ISBN 9781534199392 (hardcover) | ISBN 9781668900536 (paperback) |
   ISBN 9781668901977 (pdf) | ISBN 9781668906293 (ebook)
Subjects: LCSH: Buddhism—Juvenile literature. | CYAC: Buddhism—Essence, genius, nature—
   Juvenile literature.
Classification: LCC BQ4032 .B73 2022 | DDC 294.3—dc23
LC record available at https://lccn.loc.gov/2021039873

Printed in the United States of America
Corporate Graphics

ABOUT THE AUTHOR:

Fleur Bradley is originally from the Netherlands. She likes to travel and learn about different cultures whenever she can. Fleur has written many stories for kids and educational books. She now lives in Colorado with her family.

TABLE OF CONTENTS

Did you know? There are many image types of Buddha. This includes the Laughing Buddha and the curly-haired Buddha—except the curls are actually snails!

Introduction

Religions are systems of faith and worship. Do you have a religion? About 80 percent of the world's population does. That's 4 out of 5 people.

Every religion is different. Some have one God. That's called **monotheism**. Other religions have multiple gods. This is called **polytheism**. Some religions have an **icon** instead of a god. An icon is an important figure. Buddhism has an icon.

Buddhism is the world's fifth largest religion. About 7 percent of people are Buddhist. Almost 99 percent of Buddhists live in Asia. They live in China, Japan, Myanmar, and Thailand. They also live in Cambodia, India, Malaysia, South Korea, Sri Lanka, and Vietnam.

Buddhists believe in Buddha. The Buddha is an icon. He was the founder of Buddhism. He was a teacher. He was a philosopher. Philosophers are people who study knowledge. They study about right and wrong. The Buddha was born as Siddhartha Gautama. He was born in what is now Nepal. He was a prince. He didn't leave the palace until age 29. When he left the palace, he realized there was a lot of suffering in the world. He wondered why people grew old, got sick, and died.

Siddhartha was so upset by this that he wandered for 6 years. He decided to **meditate**. Meditating means clearing your mind. He hoped to find peace.

Siddhartha found **enlightenment** when he sat under a large fig tree. Finding enlightenment means finding the truth about life. Siddhartha became the Buddha through enlightenment. *Buddha* means "the Enlightened One" in **Sanskrit**. Sanskrit is a very old language.

Did you know? Anyone can become a Buddha.
A Buddha is someone who has reached enlightenment.

The Buddha believed that a person could reach enlightenment by letting go of their worldly desires. Worldly desires are things such as a good job or money. Nirvana is reached when these desires are let go. Nirvana is the state of enlightenment. Nirvana is the ultimate goal of a Buddhist.

The understanding of suffering and detachment is called dharma. Dharma represents the teachings of Buddhism.

THE DALAI LAMA

The Dalai Lama is a special teacher and leader who is believed by Buddhists to be reincarnated. Reincarnation means a person is born again into a new body and life. Buddhists believe that the Dalai Lama is a reincarnated god of compassion. This means when he dies, he is reborn again. It is up to the Buddhist leaders to find him again. The current Dalai Lama was found when he was 2 years old. He is the fourteenth Dalai Lama.

The current Dalai Lama had to escape Tibet as a young man in the 1950s. He was fleeing Chinese soldiers. China had a communist government. Under communism, all property belongs to the government and religion is discouraged. Chinese Communists destroyed thousands of monasteries. A monastery is where monks, or religious people, live. The Chinese Communists killed more than 100,000 Buddhist monks and nuns. The Communists wanted to wipe out Buddhism.

The Dalai Lama continues to spread the Buddhist principles of peace. He hopes to end the Chinese occupation and one day return to Tibet.

The 2 largest branches of Buddhism are **Theravada** and **Mahayana**.

Theravada Buddhists believe that enlightenment or nirvana is difficult for regular people to achieve. They believe that rebirth as a **monk** or **nun** is what's necessary to achieve enlightenment. Monks and nuns are people who take a religious vow. A vow is a promise.

Mahayana Buddhists focus on selfless work during their lifetime. They believe a regular person can reach nirvana if they follow the Buddhist path. The focus of Mahayana Buddhism is on helping others reach enlightenment.

Monica
American Buddhist

CHAPTER 1
AN AMERICAN BUDDHIST

"There aren't many Buddhists like me in the United States. Only 1 percent of the U.S. population is Buddhist," I say in front of my eighth-grade class. I'm doing a school presentation on Buddhism. The class is silent. I'm really nervous.

I take a breath.

"This is the Buddha," I say. I point to the picture. I hope no one sees how nervous I am!

I tell the class all about him.

My friend Evan asks, "So he was a regular person?"

Is there a Buddhist meditation center or temple in your area? What activities and celebrations are held there?

"Yes," I say. I feel a little less nervous now. "Well, he was a prince. So maybe not *exactly* a regular person."

The class laughs.

Next, I tell everyone about our meditation center.

"On Sundays and sometimes during the week, my family and I visit our local Buddhist meditation center. There's even a teen group. I spend a lot of time looking for ways to help others. Many other Buddhists do this in our city."

"Sounds a lot like my church's youth group!" Evan says. He smiles. "Maybe your teen group and my youth group can volunteer together."

Monica's friend Evan talks about how Buddhism has some similarities to his religion. If you practice a religion, can you think of ways your faiths are similar? How are they different?

Did you know? The majority of Buddhists in the United States identify as White or Asian.

"That's a great idea, Evan," says our teacher, Mr. Jones.

I smile too. I'm happy my friends want to learn more about my faith.

Now all of my nervousness is gone. Just in time for the lunch bell.

Did you know? Hawaii has the most Buddhists by percentage. About 8 percent of the people in Hawaii identify as Buddhists.

CHAPTER 2
A BUDDHIST CELEBRATION

I'm so relieved my presentation is over! I rush to catch up with my friends at our lunch table.

"You did so great," my friend Kristen says. "That was really interesting."

Evan nods. "The Buddha is pretty cool."

I laugh. "Yes, he is." I unpack my lunch. I usually bring a vegetarian wrap from home.

"Is that why you're a vegetarian?" Kristen asks. She points at my lunch.

I nod. "Buddhists are not supposed to harm any living thing. I don't eat meat."

Kristen studies my wrap. "That looks really tasty."

"Better than what I'm having," my other friend Jamil says. He looks at his food with a frown.

"What are you doing this weekend?" Evan asks.

"We're celebrating Songkran," I say. I take a bite of my wrap. "That's our New Year's Day."

"But it's April," Jamil says. He looks confused.

I laugh. "We use the lunar calendar. That means we look at the moon's cycles for our holidays," I say. I put away my lunch box. "Songkran is really fun. We bathe our Buddha statues in water. We splash each other with water for good luck."

"Like a water balloon fight!" Jamil says.

"Only without the balloons," I laugh. "But yes. It's a really fun celebration."

Can you think of why Buddhists splash water on Songkran? What does it represent?

Did you know? Similar to Buddhist monks, many Buddhist nuns also shave their heads.

"It sounds pretty fun," Kristen says.

"I'm looking forward to it," I add.

I'm proud of my religion. I can't wait for Songkran this weekend!

Eshin
Thai Buddhist

CHAPTER 3
A YOUNG BUDDHIST IN THAILAND

My name is Eshin, and I'm a Buddhist. I live in Thailand with my family.

I start my day by meditating. Meditating means clearing your mind of all distractions. My family has a special space set up with a statue of the Buddha. Meditating is difficult because my thoughts wander often. I'm working hard to get better.

Sometimes if I have trouble meditating, I think of the Four Noble Truths. They are the teachings of the Buddha.

The first truth is that all life has some form of suffering, called **duhkha**.

The second truth is that desire causes suffering. In my case, that's a book or video game or something else I really want.

The third truth is that we end suffering by ending desire.

The fourth truth is that it's possible to get rid of this desire and find enlightenment. You have to follow the Noble Eightfold Path to do this.

When I meditate, I think of how I can follow this path—but not today. My meditation is cut short. There is a big day ahead for me!

Today is Dharma Day. That's when we celebrate the day that the Buddha first shared his teachings. I'm excited. My family and I have lots of special celebrations planned.

After breakfast, I wait for my family to get ready. I'm not just excited about Dharma Day. Tomorrow I am going to be joining the monastery for several months. I'm nervous and happy.

My little sister Daunphen pulls my hair and laughs. Tomorrow my head will be shaved to prepare me as a young monk. First, we all walk into town. That's where we visit our **wat**, which is our Buddhist temple. It's cared for by local monks.

THE NOBLE EIGHTFOLD PATH

The Noble Eightfold Path is thought by Buddhists to end desire and suffering:

1. Understanding: Know the Four Noble Truths

2. Thought: Think kind thoughts about yourself and others

3. Speech: Speak kindly; do not lie and do not use cruel words

4. Deeds: Protect others and care for nature

5. Work: Work in a way that does not harm the environment or other living creatures

6. Effort: Be positive and always do your best

7. Mindfulness: Pay attention to what you are doing; do not daydream

8. Concentration: Focus on one thing at a time

Did you know? Vesak is a Buddhist festival celebrating Buddha's birthday. Celebrations include lantern festivals and decorating temples.

We give offerings like flowers, a candle, and **incense**. Incense is like a candle. It releases a smell when burned. Our family listens to sermons of Buddhist teachings by the wat's monks. Daunphen has trouble sitting still because she's so young. I'm doing my best to meditate. I chant the Buddha's teachings.

In the evening, we have a feast with the whole family. We are vegetarians to follow the Buddha's teachings of not harming living beings. My mother is a great cook. The evening is fun.

I'm still very nervous for tomorrow though.

Monica and Eshin are both Buddhists, but they live in different countries. How is Monica's experience in the United States different from Eshin's? How is it similar?

Did you know? Buddhist monks and nuns shave their head as a sign of humility. Humility means being humble.

CHAPTER 4

BECOMING A YOUNG MONK

I could barely sleep last night. I'm so excited! This morning, I meditated. But it was so very hard to clear my mind.

My mother dresses me in a traditional saffron robe just like the Buddha himself wore. I travel by horse into our town. That's to mimic the Buddha's travels after his enlightenment. We go to the wat.

Then a monk shaves my head. It feels funny at first. But it makes the transition real. Even Daunphen is quiet. Everyone knows this is a big moment. I will join the monastery for the next few months during our rainy season called Vassa. The monastery is a simple environment.

I don't mind it. Sometimes the young monks at the monastery get to play games—even soccer!

Some of the boys are here for life. Not me. I'll rejoin my family in a few months. Don't tell Daunphen, but I miss playing with her. I miss my mother's cooking too.

The rest of the days, we read sacred texts called **Tripitaka**. The first is Vinaya Pitaka. This one has the rules for monks like me. The second is Sutta Pitaka. The third is Abhidhamma Pitaka. I won't be able to read them all in my time here.

I'm working hard to be the best Buddhist I can. Some of the monks here work on copying the sacred texts. This is so the texts won't be lost and can be used by future Buddhists.

I attempt to meditate again. I'm actually getting better at clearing my mind every day. We read and chant the holy writings. Sometimes we beg in the community with our begging bowl. This is so we can support the wat. Begging also teaches us to be humble.

BUDDHIST HOLIDAYS

Buddhists follow a lunar calendar. That means holidays don't always fall on the same date. Not all Buddhists celebrate the same holidays. Here is a quick overview of possible holidays:

Sangha Day: A festival in March. It celebrates the Buddhist community and its monks and nuns.

Songkran: Celebrated in April. It's a festival to celebrate the start of the new year. Everyone splashes each other with water for good luck.

Vesak: A holiday in May. It celebrates Buddha's birth as Siddhartha Gautama, his enlightenment, and death.

Dharma Day: A holiday in July for Theravada Buddhists. It celebrates the first sermon made by the Buddha.

Madhu Purnima: A holiday in August or September. It celebrates unity and charity. People bring honey to shrines.

SACRED TEXTS

There are many Buddhist sacred texts called sutras. But there is no central text for all. Each sect uses different texts. They are passed on by monks who painstakingly copy them by hand.

Theravada Buddhists read early copies of a sacred text called Tripitaka. Mahayana Buddhists also use this text. They also reference later texts called Mahayana Sutras. Each contains thousands of the Buddha's teachings.

I hope to travel to Bodh Gaya in India someday. This is the birthplace of Buddhism. The Mahabodhi Temple stands here. It's where Buddhists believe the Buddha achieved enlightenment. He was under a very old fig tree called the Bodhi tree.

"Right, I forgot," I say to myself. I shake my head, hoping that helps clear my thoughts. I need to focus on meditating.

Eshin's time at the monastery can be described as a rite of passage. That's something a young person does before being considered a young adult. Can you think of examples of rites of passage in your culture or religion?

ACTIVITY

MEDITATION

Buddhists practice meditation. Many people who are not Buddhist also practice meditation. It helps focus the mind. It also creates a sense of calm.

TRY MEDITATION YOURSELF:

1. Find a quiet place to sit.
2. Close your eyes.
3. Clear your mind of all thoughts. Focus on breathing slowly in and out.
4. Your mind may wander. Bring it back to focus. Clear it of all distractions.

Try meditating for 5 to 10 minutes at first. You can increase the time once you get more practice.

TIMELINE of MAJOR EVENTS

563 BCE: Birth of Siddhartha Gautama, who later became the Buddha

485–475 BCE: The first Buddhist Council takes place

260 BCE: The Indian king Ashoka Maurya becomes a Buddhist

200 BCE–200 CE: Sacred Buddhist texts, the Tripitaka and Mahayana Sutras, are written

First Century: China sees Buddhist conversions; the first Buddha statues appear

500s: Buddhism spreads to Japan

700s: The Leshan Giant Buddha statue appears in China

1959: The Dalai Lama and his followers flee Tibet following Chinese Communist invasion

2007: Buddhist monks protest government abuse in Burma; many are arrested

LEARN MORE

FURTHER READING

Loh-Hagan, Virginia. *Be Still: Practicing Meditation.* Ann Arbor, MI: Cherry Lake Publishing, 2020.

Marsico, Katie. *Buddhism.* Ann Arbor, MI: Cherry Lake Publishing, 2017.

WEBSITES

Buddhism for Kids:
https://buddhismforkids.net/facts.html

Encyclopedia Britannica Kids:
https://kids.britannica.com/kids/article/Buddhism/352887

GLOSSARY

dharma (DAHR-muh) the understanding of suffering and detachment of desires

duhkha (DAH-kuh) suffering, the path of suffering

enlightenment (ihn-LYE-tuhn-muhnt) when a Buddhist embraces the Four Noble Truths and finds nirvana

icon (EYE-kahn) an important figure

incense (IHN-senss) a substance burned to produce a fragrant scent, often used in meditation

Mahayana (mah-huh-YAH-nuh) one of the two main branches of Buddhism; its followers believe it is possible for a regular person to reach nirvana through selfless work

meditate (MEH-duh-tayt) to clear one's mind to find calm and enlightenment

monk (MOHNK) a man who takes a vow to serve his religion; most monks live in monasteries

monotheism (mah-nuh-THEE-ih-zuhm) a religion that believes in one God

nirvana (nir-VAH-nuh) the ultimate goal of enlightenment in Buddhism

nun (NUHN) a woman who takes a vow to serve her religion

polytheism (PAH-lee-thee-ih-zuhm) a religion that believes in multiple gods

Sanskrit (SAHN-skrit) an ancient language used for most Buddhist texts

Theravada (ther-uh-VAH-duh) one of the two main branches in Buddhism; its followers believe it's hard for regular people to reach nirvana; regular people achieve enlightenment through rebirth as a monk or nun

Tripitaka (trih-puh-TAH-kuh) the earliest collection of Buddhist written teachings

wat (WAHT) a monastery in Thailand

INDEX